Native Americans

The Creek

Barbara A. Gray-Kanatiiosh

ABDO Publishing Company

visit us at
www.abdopub.com

Published by ABDO Publishing Company, 4940 Viking Drive, Suite 622, Edina, Minnesota 55435. Copyright © 2002 Abdo Consulting Group, Inc. International copyrights reserved in all countries. No part of this book may be reproduced in any form without written permission from the publisher.

Printed in the United States.

Illustrations: David Kanietakeron Fadden
Cover Photo: Deborah Doiron
Interior Photos: Corbis
Editors: Bob Italia, Tamara L. Britton, Kate A. Furlong, Kristin Van Cleaf
Book Design & Graphics: Neil Klinepier

Library of Congress Cataloging-in-Publication Data

Gray-Kanatiiosh, Barbara A., 1963-
    The Creek / Barbara A. Gray-Kanatiiosh.
       p. cm. -- (Native Americans)
   Includes bibliographical references and index.
   Summary: Introduces the crafts, myths, and modern and traditional way of life of the native Americans known as the Muscogee, or Creek, whose homelands were in what is now Georgia and Alabama.
    ISBN 1-57765-605-9
   1. Creek Indians--History--Juvenile literature. 2. Creek Indians--Social life and customs--Juvenile literature. [1. Creek Indians. 2. Indians of North America.] I. Title. II. Native Americans (Edina, Minn.)

E99.C9 G69 2002
975.004'973--dc21

2001056493

About the Author: Barbara A. Gray-Kanatiiosh, JD

Barbara Gray-Kanatiiosh, JD, is an Akwesasne Mohawk. She has a Juris Doctorate from Arizona State University, where she was one of the first recipients of ASU's special certificate in Indian Law. She is currently pursuing a Ph.D. in Justice Studies at ASU and is focusing on Native American issues. Barbara works hard to educate children about Native Americans through her writing and Web site where children may ask questions and receive a written response about the Haudenosaunee culture. The Web site is: www.peace4turtleisland.org

Illustrator: David Kanietakeron Fadden

David Kanietakeron Fadden is a member of the Akwesasne Mohawk Wolf Clan. His work has appeared in publications such as *Akwesasne Notes, Indian Time*, and the *Northeast Indian Quarterly*. Examples of his work have also appeared in various publications of the Six Nations Indian Museum in Onchiota, NY. His work has also appeared in "How The West Was Lost: Always The Enemy," produced by Gannett Production, which appeared on the Discovery Channel. David's work has been exhibited in Albany, NY; the Lake Placid Center for the Arts; Centre Strathearn in Montreal, Quebec; North Country Community College in Saranac Lake, NY; Paul Smith's College in Paul Smiths, NY; and at the Unison Arts & Learning Center in New Paltz, NY.

Contents

Where They Lived 4
Society 6
Homes 8
Food 10
Clothing 12
Crafts 14
Family 16
Children 18
Myths 20
War 22
Contact with Europeans 24
Chitto Harjo 26
The Creek Today 28
Glossary 31
Web Sites 31
Index 32

Where They Lived

The Creek traditionally lived in the southeastern region of the United States. Their homelands spread across present-day Georgia and Alabama. Those who lived in present-day Georgia were called Lower Creeks. Those who lived in present-day Alabama were called Upper Creeks.

Creek homelands had many different features. Some areas contained mountains, forests, hills, valleys, rivers, lakes, and creeks. Other areas had marshes and swamps where birds, alligators, and poisonous snakes lived.

A stream running through the Creek traditional homelands in Georgia

The Creek received their name from European settlers. The settlers traded with Native Americans who lived near a part of the Ocmulgee River that the settlers called Ochesee Creek. The traders soon began calling these Native Americans the Creek. But the Creek call themselves Muscogee.

The Creek Traditional Homelands

Society

The Creek society was made up of several **clans**. They included Wind, Skunk, Beaver, Bear, Wolf, Bird, Fox, Panther, Wildcat, Potato, Alligator, Raccoon, Toad, and Deer clans. The clans linked people to each other and to the Natural World.

The Creek clans lived in large, permanent towns. At least one *micco* (MEEK-koh), or chief, led each town. He was a respected man whom the people selected. He made decisions for the town with the help of advisers.

Each town had a political and ceremonial center. In the center stood a large council house, a town square, and a large U-shaped field. Meetings, dances, games, and other ceremonial events took place there.

Creek towns were divided into red towns and white towns. The red towns were home to warriors. The white towns were home to peacemakers.

Opposite page: A Creek town

Homes

Creek homes surrounded the ceremonial center of the town. Each family had a plot of land. Each plot had room for several buildings. Some buildings stored food, others served as winter homes, and still others served as summer homes.

Winter and summer homes were rectangular. Winter homes had wooden frames and roofs woven out of vines and branches. The Creek plastered these structures with mud. The mud kept the heat inside during the winter. These homes had no windows. But there was a smoke hole in each roof.

Summer homes also had wooden frames. The frames held up thatched roofs. The Creek made the roofs by tying dried grass to the frames. These homes kept the people comfortable by letting in the cool night air.

The food storage buildings were usually two stories tall. They held baskets and containers filled with dried meat, fish, corn, and other foods. The Creek also stored their tools in these buildings.

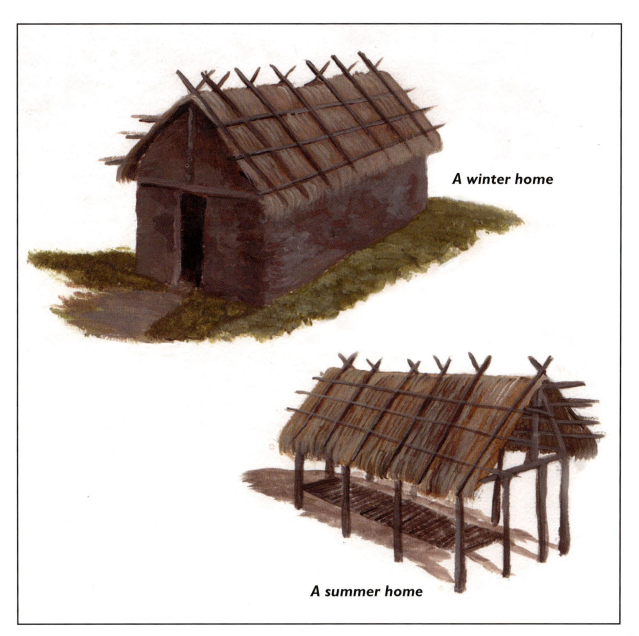

A winter home

A summer home

Food

The Creek gathered, hunted, fished, and farmed. They gathered berries, nuts, herbs, and wild onions. They hunted deer, alligators, bears, rabbits, squirrels, ducks, doves, and bobwhite quail. The Creek hunted with bows and arrows, blowguns made from cane, and woven **snares**.

Creek homelands contained many rivers filled with fish. The Creek caught trout, bass, and catfish. They fished with spears and lines tied to bone hooks. They also used woven twig fences to trap fish in shallow water.

The Creek grew corn, squash, beans, sweet potatoes, and pumpkins. They used hoes and planting sticks. The hoe was made from stone, or from a deer's shoulder bone attached to a long stick.

Deer meat and corn were the Creek's most important foods. The Creek stored the food they could not eat right away. They dried meat, fish, berries, and vegetables to eat in the winter.

The Creek washed corn with **lye** and made a soup called *sofkey*. Sometimes they pounded corn into meal with a **mortar** and **pestle**. Then they mixed the cornmeal with beans and made it into cakes.

A Creek man using a blowgun

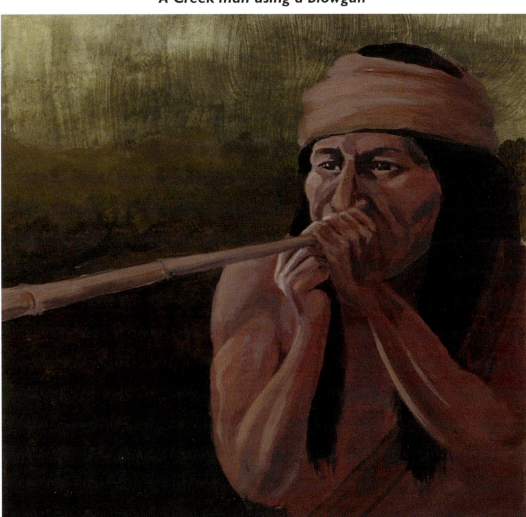

Clothing

The Creek made clothing from deerskins, plant fibers, and animal furs. Women used **awls**, bone needles, and **sinew** to make clothing.

Men wore deerskin **breechcloths** and **leggings**. They wore **sashes** that hung over one shoulder and tied at the waist. The sashes were woven from plant fibers.

Women wore deerskin dresses and skirts. They made these dresses by sewing two deer **hides** together. Women wore tops woven from plant fibers and rabbit fur. They also wore woven sashes.

Both men and women wore deerskin moccasins. They wore shawls woven from grass over their shoulders. To keep warm in the winter, they wore fur robes.

Men **tattooed** their chests and faces. Sometimes they painted their faces, too. They made the face paint from minerals and plants. They also wore turbans on their heads. Sometimes they placed feathers in their turbans. They also wore earrings and necklaces.

A Creek family in traditional clothing

Crafts

The Creek made beautiful, finger-woven **sashes**, belts, and cloth. To do this, they rolled plant fibers such as cotton, Indian hemp, and milkweed into strings. Sometimes they dyed the strings with plants and berries.

The women tied strings to a small, horizontal twig. They wove the strings back and forth to make a sash. Sometimes they wove designs into the sashes. The designs might include **geometric** shapes, or designs such as lightning.

The Creek made a special sash with a square pouch. The pouch had a triangular-shaped flap. They wore the sash over one shoulder. The pouch hung right below the waist. The sashes and pouches were **embroidered** with scroll designs. The scroll designs represented the Creator's breath.

After Europeans arrived in Creek homelands, the Creek began using trade goods to make and decorate their clothing. These goods included wool cloth and glass beads.

A Creek man wears an embroidered sash and pouch.

Family

Clans were important to Creek society. Clans brought people together as one big family. The Creek had a matrilineal society. This means that children belonged to the clan of their mother.

The Creek had to "marry across the fire." This meant they could not marry someone from their own clan. People of the same clan, whether related by blood or not, were considered family.

When a man wanted to marry a woman, he gave her a gift. If she took the gift, that meant she agreed to marry him. Then the man moved into the woman's home. If the couple still wanted to marry after a year passed, a wedding was held. Once married, the man continued to live in his wife's family home.

Each person in the family had a role. Women tended to the children and the farming. They also prepared food and made clothing. Men hunted, fished, made tools, and protected the people. Older men and women kept the Creek history and stories alive. They taught the children traditional ceremonies, songs, dances, and stories.

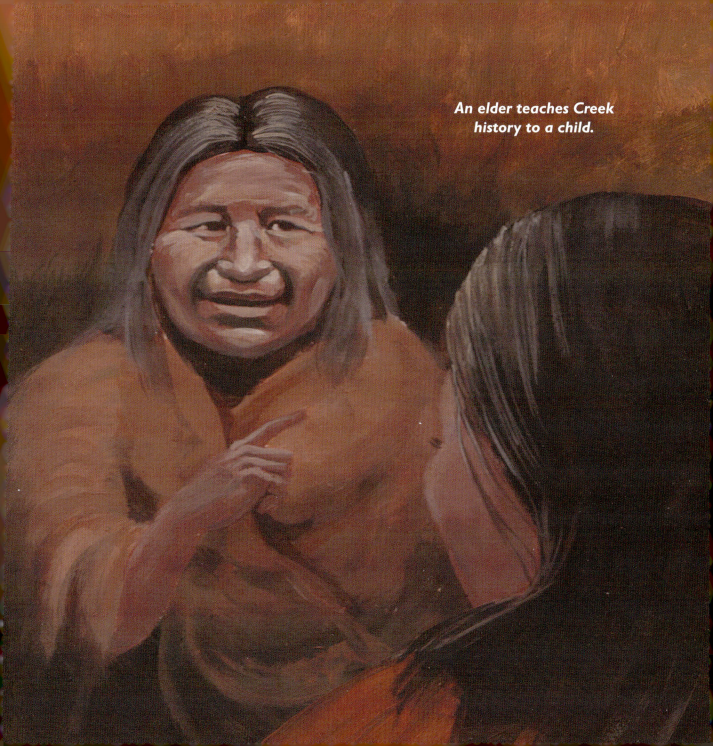

An elder teaches Creek history to a child.

Children

Children learned skills from their mothers' sisters and brothers. Uncles taught the boys, and aunts taught the girls. This brought the extended family closer.

The uncles taught the boys many skills, such as how to hunt and fish. Boys learned how to make blowguns for hunting. They also watched the men make dugout canoes.

Girls helped care for younger children. They learned how to sew and finger weave. They helped their aunts prepare foods, such as corn dumplings and deer jerky.

Grandparents told stories to the children. Some stories made everyone laugh. Other stories were serious, and taught the children lessons about Creek life.

Creek children also enjoyed playing games, such as chunky. To play chunky, one player rolled a round stone down the playing field. The other players threw long sticks to where they thought the stone would stop.

Playing chunky taught young Creek how to throw spears accurately.

Myths

The Creek believe the Creator made them from red earth. Soon after creation, the Creek crawled out of the Earth's mouth. When they reached the top, they spread out in every direction like ants.

The Creator sent a blanket of fog over the earth. The fog blinded the Creek. They stopped, and called out to each other. By following the sounds of their voices, the Creek found each other.

Then the Creator stood in the east near the rising sun. He took a deep breath and blew the fog away. He said to the Creek, "Now you see how important it is to stay together. The first thing you see will be your **clan**. All members of your clan will be family."

The Creek standing closest to the sun called themselves the Wind clan. They were the first to see the wind blow away the fog. Then each group saw things such as a panther, a snake, a potato, or an alligator. This is how each clan got its name.

The Creek call the Creator the Master-of-Breath, because he blew the fog away. He also taught the Creek an important lesson about family.

The Creator blows away the fog.

War

The Creek usually went to war to avenge the killing of one of their people. They also fought to protect their lands.

In battle, Creek warriors used blowguns, bows and arrows, knives, war clubs, and spears. The men often wore shell or bone **gorgets** on their necks. The gorgets protected their necks and chests from arrows and knives during battle. After they began to trade with Europeans, the Creek also used guns in battle.

In the early 1800s, a Shawnee chief named Tecumseh visited the Creek. He convinced some of them to join with northern tribes to fight against white settlers. These Creek warriors were called Red Sticks.

On August 30, 1813, the Red Sticks attacked Fort Mims. They killed several hundred men, women, and children. U.S. General Andrew Jackson led troops on several attacks against the Creek. The most important was the Battle of Horseshoe Bend in 1814. The Creek lost this battle. They were forced to give 23 million acres of their homelands to the United States.

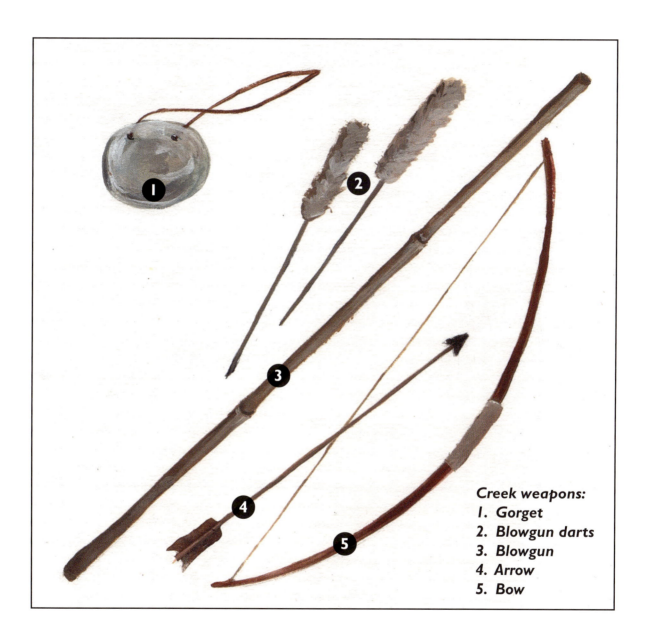

Contact with Europeans

The first contact between the Creek and Europeans was around 1540. During this time, Spanish explorer Hernando de Soto passed through Creek territory. The Creek traded with the Spanish for iron tools such as axes, hoes, and **adzes**.

In 1670, the English built Charles Town on Creek homelands. Charles Town became a trading center for the English and Creek. The English wanted deerskins, which they shipped to England to be made into leather items. In exchange for deerskins, the Creek got cloth, glass beads, tin pots and pans, tools, guns, and ammunition.

Soon, some Creek warriors began changing their traditional ways. The English wanted Native Americans to sell as slaves in the colonies. So some Creek made war on other tribes to take captives. They traded the captives to the English for goods.

In 1830, the Indian Removal Act became law. It called for all Native Americans living east of the Mississippi River to move to Indian Territory. It was located in the present-day state of Oklahoma.

Some Creek moved to Indian Territory. Others stayed on **allotments** in their traditional homelands. But beginning in 1836, the U.S. government forced most of the remaining Creek to march to Indian Territory. Many died on the journey. Some Creek hid in the swamps. Others traveled south to live with the Seminole.

A Creek man and a settler trade at Charles Town.

Chitto Harjo

Chitto Harjo (chit-toe ha-cho) was a Creek chief. His name means Recklessly Brave Snake. But settlers called him Crazy Snake.

Harjo fought to preserve the traditional Creek **culture**. He was against the General **Allotment** Act. This act was designed to break up tribally owned lands and Native American traditions. Chitto Harjo saw this act as a threat to his culture.

Chitto Harjo and his followers also thought the General Allotment Act broke the Treaty of 1832. This treaty had promised the Creek self-government. So in the winter of 1900, he and his followers set up a traditional Creek government in a town called Hickory Ground.

In the spring of 1901, U.S. troops raided Hickory Ground. They broke up the Creek government. Many of the people involved in the government received long prison terms.

Despite this, Chitto Harjo continued to speak against **allotment**. He and his followers traveled to Washington, D.C., several times to speak before the U.S. Congress.

At a special session of the Senate in 1906, Chitto Harjo told the history between the Creek and the U.S. government. He reminded the lawmakers about the treaties that promised the Creek the right to self-government. Despite Chitto Harjo's efforts, Congress did not make any changes to its allotment policies.

Chitto Harjo

The Creek Today

Today, there are two Creek **reservations**. The Muscogee (Creek) Nation is located in east-central Oklahoma. This reservation has more than 44,000 enrolled members. In 1984, the Poarch **Band** of Creek Indians, in Alabama, became a federally recognized tribe. Today, they have about 1,840 members.

Marian McCormick, principal chief of the Lower Muscogee Creek Tribe, holds a gallberry broom at tribal headquarters near Whigham, Georgia, on May 30, 2001. Her ancestors hid in a swamp to avoid being sent to an Oklahoma reservation.

The Creek people are working to retain their language and **culture**. Many Creek children learn their language in public schools. The people also gather for ceremonial dances.

Today, stomp dances are held monthly from May until September. At ceremonies, people dance, sing, and have fun. They play stickball and eat traditional foods.

Julia Wakeford, 3, dances in the Fancy Shawl for Juniors Dance. She is from Tulsa, Oklahoma, representing the Muscogee tribe during the Intertribal Pow Wow. The Pow Wow was held at Memorial Coliseum in Corpus Christi, Texas, September 26, 1999.

An important celebration is the Green Corn Ceremony. During this ceremony, the people give thanks for their harvests. There are speeches and dances. Women do a stomp dance, where they wear turtle shell rattles or cans around their ankles. The shells and cans make music. A sacred fire is lit. People leave the ceremony feeling spiritually fed and happy.

Today, the Creek live all over the world. They have many types of jobs. For example, Joy Harjo is a Creek poet and musician. She plays the saxophone in a band.

"Butch" McIntosh, a Creek Native American, is a Fancy Dancer. He performed the Fancy War Dance in the Oklahoma Masonic Indian Degree Team Dance on April 9, 1999.

Glossary

adze - a tool that looks like an ax. It is used for trimming and shaping wood.
allotment - a plot of land owned by an individual. The U.S. government's allotment policies ended the Creek's tradition of community land ownership.
awl - a pointed tool for marking or making small holes in materials such as leather or wood.
breechcloth - a piece of hide or cloth, usually worn by men, that was wrapped between the legs and tied with a belt around the waist.
clan - a group of families in a community that has a common ancestor.
culture - the customs, arts, and tools of a nation or people at a certain time.
embroider - to decorate cloth or leather with a pattern of stitches.
geometric - made up of straight lines, circles, and other simple shapes.
gorget - a piece of armor used to protect the throat.
hide - an animal skin that is often thick and heavy.
leggings - coverings for the legs, usually made of cloth or leather.
lye - a strong solution obtained from wood ashes.
mortar - a strong bowl or cup in which a material is pounded.
pestle - a club-shaped tool used to pound and crush something.
reservation - a piece of land set aside by the government for Native Americans to live on.
sash - a wide piece of cloth used like a belt.
sinew - a band of tough fibers that joins a muscle to a bone.
snare - a trap for catching small animals. Snares usually have a noose that tightens around an animal's legs when it enters the trap.
tattoo - to permanently mark the skin with figures or designs.

Web Sites

Muscogee (Creek) Nation of Oklahoma: http://www.ocevnet.org/creek/index.html

The Poarch Band of Creek Indians: http://www.poarchcreekindians.org/

These sites are subject to change. Go to your favorite search engine and type in Creek for more sites.

Index

A
Alabama 4, 28
allotment 25, 26, 27

C
ceremonies 6, 8, 16, 29, 30
Charles Town 24
children 16, 18, 29
Chitto Harjo 26, 27
clans 6, 16, 20
clothing 12, 14, 16
Congress, U.S. 27
crafts 14

D
dances 6, 16, 29, 30
de Soto, Hernando 24

E
Europeans 5, 14, 22, 24

F
farming 10, 16
fishing 10, 16, 18
food 8, 10, 11, 16, 18, 29, 30
Fort Mims 22

G
games 6, 18, 29
gathering 10
General Allotment Act 26
Georgia 4
Green Corn Ceremony 30

H
Harjo, Joy 30
Hickory Ground 26
homelands 4, 5, 10, 14, 22, 24, 25
homes 8
Horseshoe Bend, Battle of 22
hunting 10, 16, 18

I
Indian Territory 24, 25
Indian Removal Act 24

J
Jackson, Andrew 22

M
marriage 16
Muscogee 5
Muscogee (Creek) Nation 28

O
Ochesee Creek 5
Ocmulgee River 5
Oklahoma 24, 28

P
Poarch Band of Creek Indians 28

R
Red Sticks 22
red towns 6
reservations 28

S
Seminole 25
slavery 24

T
Tecumseh 22
tools 8, 10, 11, 12, 16, 24
towns 6, 8
trade 5, 14, 22, 24
Treaty of 1832 26

W
war 22, 24
Washington, D.C. 27
weapons 10, 18, 22, 24
weaving 12, 14, 18
white towns 6